Comanche
Warriors

By David Schach

BELLWETHER MEDIA • MINNEAPOLIS, MN

TM

Are you ready to take it to the extreme?
Torque books thrust you into the action-packed world
of sports, vehicles, mystery, and adventure. These books
may include dirt, smoke, fire, and dangerous stunts.
Warning: read at your own risk.

Library of Congress Cataloging-in-Publication Data

Schach, David.
 Comanche warriors / by David Schach.
    p. cm. -- (Torque: history's greatest warriors)
 Includes bibliographical references and index.
 Summary: "Engaging images accompany information about Comanche warriors. The combination of
high-interest subject matter and light text is intended for students in grades 3 through 7"--Provided by
publisher.
 ISBN 978-1-60014-628-2 (hardcover : alk. paper)
 1. Comanche Indians--Wars--Juvenile literature. 2. Indian weapons--Great Plains--Juvenile literature.
3. Comanche Indians--History--Juvenile literature. I. Title.
 E99.C85S32 2011
 978.004'974572--dc22   2011004212

This edition first published in 2012 by Bellwether Media, Inc.

Printed in the United States of America, North Mankato, MN.

080111   1187

Contents

Who Were Comanche Warriors?

Comanche warriors were Native American **braves** who belonged to the Comanche tribe. The Comanche lived on the **Great Plains** of North America. They hunted buffalo with bows and arrows. They used these animals for food, clothing, and shelter. The Comanche guarded the buffalo in their territory from other tribes. Comanche warriors attacked anyone who **trespassed** on their land.

Comanche warriors were skilled hand-to-hand fighters. In the 1700s, European **settlers** brought horses with them to North America. The Comanche quickly mastered horse training and riding. Their skills on horseback made them feared throughout the Great Plains.

Horses gave Comanche warriors an advantage in battle. Warriors could quickly surround enemies and fire arrows from horseback. They easily conquered other tribes and increased their territory.

Comanche Fact

The Ute tribe gave the Comanche their name. The Comanche call themselves *Numinu*, which means "the people."

The Comanche and His Warhorse

Each Comanche warrior had his own warhorse. It was called his "eternity horse."

Spanish Mustangs

This breed was the most common eternity horse. They were considered sacred.

Medicine Hat

These horses had white markings on their head. The Comanche believed they made warriors invincible.

The Warrior Afterlife

Comanche warriors believed they joined their eternity horses after death. They would ride together forever, feeling no pain, hunger, or thirst.

Comanche Warrior Training

Every Comanche boy trained to be a warrior. Training focused on riding horses and using bows and arrows. Boys learned to ride horses as early as age 5. They soon began shooting arrows from horseback. Later, they learned to pick up objects while at a **gallop**.

Young Comanche had to show their bravery and skill to adult warriors. They went hunting with the warriors and had to kill a buffalo. Then they joined a **raiding party**. When the party attacked, the young Comanche had to kill enemies and capture horses. They became warriors once they passed these tests.

Comanche Fact

Comanche warriors often surprised their enemies by attacking under the light of a full moon. People throughout the Great Plains began to use the term "Comanche Moon" because of these raids.

Comanche Warrior Weapons and Gear

Comanche warriors brought a variety of weapons into battle. They used most of their weapons from horseback. The main Comanche weapon was the bow and arrow. Bows were made of wood and strung with the **tendons** of buffalo. Arrowheads were made of **flint**. Feathers were attached to the ends of arrows. This helped the arrows fly straight.

bow

arrows

Hand-to-hand combat was rare in Comanche battles. Still, warriors had to be ready for it. Some rode with long, wooden lances. Others carried small axes called tomahawks. Spears and clubs were also used to bring down enemies.

spear

tomahawk

Comanche Fact

European settlers brought
guns to the Great Plains.
Skilled Comanche warriors
could fire them from horseback.

Comanche warriors did not
wear armor. It was heavy and
would slow down their horses.
Warriors sometimes carried small
shields made of deerskin and
buffalo hide. Some Comanche
warriors decorated their shields
with the **scalp** of an enemy.

The Decline of Comanche Warriors

Comanche warriors attacked almost every Native American tribe on the Great Plains. They made many enemies. Over time, their enemies fought back. There were too many for the Comanche to fight at once. By the mid-1800s, the Comanche had lost most of their territory.

The Comanche also faced other problems. Many caught diseases from European settlers. The settlers also killed many of the buffalo the Comanche needed to survive.

Comanche Fact

Quanah Parker was the chief of the last band of free Comanche. He was the son of a European woman who married a Comanche chief.

In the 1860s, the United States government tried to move all of the Comanche to a **reservation**. Comanche warriors fought back. However, the U.S. Army had more men and better weapons. In 1875, the last free Comanche warriors gave up the fight. The Comanche tribe lived on, but its fierce warriors and old way of life had come to an end.

Glossary

braves—Native American warriors

flint—a hard stone; Comanche warriors used flint to make arrowheads and spearheads for their weapons.

gallop—a medium-paced run for a horse

Great Plains—a large area of plains in central North America

raiding party—a group of warriors that attacked other tribes to capture resources

reservation—land set aside for a specific tribe of Native Americans

scalp—the skin that covers the top of the head

settlers—people who settle in a new place

tendons—cords of tissue that connect muscle to bone

trespassed—went on someone else's land without permission

To Learn More

AT THE LIBRARY

Cunningham, Kevin, and Peter Benoit.
The Comanche. New York, N.Y.: Children's Press, 2011.

Englar, Mary. *Comanche Warriors*.
Mankato, Minn.: Capstone Press, 2008.

Lacey, Theresa Jensen. *The Comanche*. New York, N.Y.:
Chelsea House, 2011.

ON THE WEB

Learning more about
Comanche warriors is as easy as 1, 2, 3.

1. Go to www.factsurfer.com.

2. Enter "Comanche warriors" into the search box.

3. Click the "Surf" button and you will see a list of
related Web sites.

With factsurfer.com, finding more information
is just a click away.

Index

The images in this book are reproduced through the courtesy of: Marilyn
Angel Wynn/Photolibrary, front cover, pp. 9, 20; George Catlin/Getty
Images, p. 4; Mark Lisk/Alamy, p. 5; Nancy G Western Photography, Nancy
Greifenhagen/Alamy, p. 7; Allen Russell/Alamy, pp. 10-11; SuperStock/Getty
Images, pp. 12-13; Marilyn Angel Wynn/Nativestock.com/Getty Images,
pp. 14-15; Juan Martinez, p. 15 (bow, arrow); SuperStock/Masterfile, p. 16;
Michael/Vigliotti, p. 17 (spear, tomahawk); Archive Image/Alamy, pp. 18-19;
U.S. Army, p. 21.